"Thank you,"

for your service to us
Veterans and congratulations
on your retirement

THROUGH *My* WINDOW

DARRYL SNODDY

THROUGH MY WINDOW

iUniverse books may be ordered through booksellers or by contacting:

iUniverse
1663 Liberty Drive
Bloomington, IN 47403
www.iuniverse.com
1-800-Authors (1-800-288-4677)

Because of the dynamic nature of the Internet, any web addresses or links contained in this book may have changed since publication and may no longer be valid. The views expressed in this work are solely those of the author and do not necessarily reflect the views of the publisher, and the publisher hereby disclaims any responsibility for them.

Any people depicted in stock imagery provided by Thinkstock are models, and such images are being used for illustrative purposes only.
Certain stock imagery © Thinkstock.

ISBN: 978-1-5320-1768-1 (sc)
ISBN: 978-1-5320-1767-4 (e)

Library of Congress Control Number: 2017905762

Print information available on the last page.

iUniverse rev. date: 05/09/2017

Listen

Let's take some time, let's listen, for the truth in what life brings.
Let go of all egoic thought; dismiss all earthly things!
Let's contemplate our spiritual lives- the lives that truly matter,
The essence of our Godly souls; let's break through all this chatter!

Just think of how we spend our days; some struggle to exist.
Collecting all these earthly things of never ending lists.
We live our lives in quest of some condition we won't find.
Disillusioned by mere concepts that are strictly of the mind.

"Someday I will be happy", are the words of those who dream.
But happy flows just like the wind —it comes and goes you see!
The things we try to hold to, are just worldly things indeed!
And time will show that worldly things are not the things we need!

"You cannot take it with you", is a spiritual phrase in grace!
Reminder of our spiritual realm where possessions have no place!
And yet, this truth, this spoken phrase, is rarely realized.
These words professed for spiritual ears, are lost in worldly eyes.

For rarely do we stand for things that remind us of our truths.
We are mindful of the things of man; like there's something there
to lose!
The truth will set you free one day— can this be meant of death?
Don't take for granted spiritual phrase, and be Blessed in spiritual
breath!

While You Were Out

While you were out
I made you this list.
I've listed the times
And the things that you missed!

I've started with New Years,
The end of the year.
You forgot to be with us,
So, that day had no cheer!

Oh, you missed our birthdays-
By the way, there were four.
Never took a look back
As you walked out our door!

And NOW, you come smiling
With your hum and your haw;
With your fancy new suit
And your fancy new car?

I can't call you Daddy,
Because that isn't your role!
And, of course, there's the fact
That these days, I'm too old!

My kids can't call you Grandpa,
So, they'll just use your name!
That's the respect that feels worthy-
All your kids feel the same!

Do you think yourself worthy
Of respect from your seeds?
When YOU chose to walk out
And never jiggled your keys!

You better take what you're given.
We're going to give you this chance!
Though, you didn't raise boys
Or have you Daughter's first dance!

There's been a lot that you've missed
In the time you've been gone!
So, we can't reminisce
If we talk on the phone!

We will try to move forward
While we hold to the past!
Not impressed by that suit
Or that car that you have!

Thou Shall Not Judge

Who appointed YOU my judge?
The one who walks on airs?
Is it you, who sets the standards?
In God's place YOU dare to stand?

And how does one come to this place,
To sit upon His throne?
The arrogance to act as if
You walk with Him alone!

You haven't got the right to judge
'Cause no man's without sin.
And though the Good Book lays the rules
Our answers are within.

See God, He may have laid the rules
To guide us 'long the way,
But through the heart, with Love abound,
He speaks to us each day.

For some, it's premonition
Or the answer to a prayer.
The truth is, God's found many ways
To let us know He's there.

We walk our lives with God along.
He's with us everyday.
And if you judge, He'll touch your heart
And this is what He'll say.

"My child, though you are in My image,
Perfection you don't own.
For no man walks in Godly shoes,
And no man shares My throne!"

So hold no man to worldly standards.
It just won't mean a thing;
When we all reach our judgement day
And stand before our King.

A Man in the Park

He woke up one morning
A man in the park.
The bright of the morning
His life in the dark.

He gathered his things.
For the man in the blue
Said that he could not stay—
Said, "Let's go you must move!"

So where will he go?
'Cause this life is so new!
He looked up to the sky
Then looked down to his shoes!

They still had that shine,
But had gathered some scuffs.
His life was so blissful.
But today, things are rough!

He looked to his left
And then looked to his right.
He queried direction
To start his new life!

Put hope in his bag.
That was all that he had!
He took a deep breath
And he let out some sad!

He pondered his life
As he looked at his hand.
It wouldn't hold much
So he looked for a can!

His pride had to fall
As he begged for some change.
He reflected through tears
As it started to rain!

Not a coin had he gathered—
With the rain went his hope!
He stood where he was
And he pondered the rope!

He cried in his moment
And the rain met his tears.
Lost the man who was hopeful—
Found the man who now fears!

Do you see where I'm going?
Do I need to say more?
Will you spare just a dollar
When he approaches your door?

Or will you find comfort
In the thoughts of your head?
Think you know this guy's story
Like some novel you've read!

This is not a true story—
Not for you or for me!
But it's someone's life now
I just want you to see!

We should not take for granted
What's before us this day!
Yesterday shoes were shiny.
I pray you keep them that way!

The Messengers

Judge me not by what is said-
By gossip's mouth, through ear.
When judgement turns upon my walk;
When it's my shoes they would wear.

If word is, I've said from my lips
Some things that do offend,
Then give me chance to say <u>My</u> words
To straighten out the bend!

Oh, how we judge through others' verse,
And lash out with the tongue;
To hold this man to judgement
For something THEY say he's done?

And why is it so easy
You'd believe from distant verse;
To judge so fast from others' words
And not come to me first!

For petty are the words of those
Who pass on words of tale.
Are postmen asked to read it first
And then give YOU your mail?

Of course not! That would be a crime.
Those words are yours to read.
Please treat my words like letters bound.
They're yours alone to heed!

Allow my words to come to pass
From MY lips to your ears.
And judge me not by words of those
Who start with: "Did you hear!"

For twisted, sometimes, is the tongue
Of those who bring you word.
And rarely is the message pure
From those who say they've heard!

And please forgive the messengers.
They know not what they do.
Hey, let's keep all the words we'll have
Between just me and you!

Intentions are not mine, to try
To break your sacred heart.
Forgive me for the times I may
Have acted out of dark.

I guess I'm trying to bring to light
The damage tongue can cause.
I ask that should they bend your ear,
You give our friendship pause.

Give pause to all the days we've shared-
The good days and the bad.
The things that only I could hear
'Bout thoughts your spirit had.

Just let our friendship stand in truth.
We've stood the test of time!
And let those fools who'd bend your ear
Reflect on what truth finds.

For Ours, is one that stands in awe
By those who see our light.
And in that light no shadows cast
By those whose tongues take flight!

Our love will stand forever more.
Our friendship's theirs to test.
What they don't see in front of "friend",
The word we use is "BEST"!

That Quiet Place

I've tried to find that quiet place.
I've looked for peace of mind.
I've searched throughout my bedroom
But there it did not hide.

I waited in my car for it;
I guess I was too late!
Because I was there for quite some time
I could no longer wait!

And Oprah said that in the tub
My silence I could find,
But Oprah must not have a kid!
At least not one like mine!

Sometimes I wonder if this place
Is given as a wish?
Because sometimes Mom, with hands on hips,
Asked for it as a gift!

Though silence I may never find
I still search every day
In hopes I'll find it long before
My butt has passed away!

P.O.W. — M.A.H.
Prisoner of War — Missing at Home

You look at me, what so you see?
A man who's lost his dignity?
A man, the slave to many drugs?
Or maybe just a pauper!

I have a name.
I had a cause.
I have a son
And daughter.

My life you see, is not my own.
This wasn't meant to be.
I lost myself in Vietnam.
A Victim's what you see!

At seventeen my country called
To go protect another.
And so I went, with flag in hand,
To fight beside my brothers.

I never thought the things I'd see
Might come to change my eyes.
In shortened time, I came to witness
Things not realized.

If not by promise to obey
The orders put before me.
I surely would have turned around
And would not have this story!

My breakfast is a bottle
And for lunch I'll have a snort.
Don't have a job; don't have a home.
My mind's all out of sorts.

"Don't bother me you bum!", I'll hear,
When I ask for some change.
I need a fix, a hit, or shot
At night to ease my pain.

For me — Please don't feel sorry,
'Cause my memories won't subside.
There's a never-ending battle
That keeps running through my mind.

Society says I'm crazy
And that I should be on meds.
As if there is a cure-all
For these visions in my head!

See, sometimes I'm in battle
And I dream of all my kills.
I wish I could forget the things
I did against my will!

I sacrificed my Family,
My body and my mind.
I went to serve my country
And I left my soul behind.

Some things I did I am ashamed
As much now, as was then.
But times were hard and we were boys
Soon thrusted to be men.

I could not have compassion.
I could not show my fear.
I just fought hard for three long years
And held back all my tears!

I slept in hardened trenches.
I crawled along the ground.
I learned to march among the dead
And sleep without a sound.

I watched my brothers die beside me.
Waited for my turn!
The only hope I ever held
Was home I might return.

And then one day my orders came.
Said I was going home!
To see again the Family
I had left back home, alone.

But things were not the same, you see.
Not as we all expected.
I could not cope with social life
And soon I was rejected.

So to these streets I laid my claim
To try to ease the pain,
Of all those Family members
Who said, "I was not the same."

I don't expect compassion.
And I don't need your parade.
I just would like remembrance
Of the sacrifices made!

Not to Be Forgotten

They say a Mom's the toughest job
That anyone could have.
I beg to differ, because I know,
It's tough to be a Dad!

A mother gets to know her child
As soon as it's conceived.
She gets to share its every move
And feed it all its meals!

We dads, we have to wait nine months
Before we get our turn!
And our first days are filled with cries,
And curses mom has learned!

But dads are men who take their job
With pride and head held high;
Who realize that their new child
Will need him by its side!

So please, don't take for granted
All the things that most dads do!
See, children need their mothers
But, they need their daddies too!

My Baby's Daddy

He's my baby's father, but she doesn't have his name!
Afraid the title Daddy might, somehow, affect his game!
I used to think that Daddy, would make fathers feel real proud,
But I have seen your father, try to get lost in a crowd.

See, I have seen the blessing, in the gift I have in you!
I really wish your father, could feel blessed the way I do!
I know I cannot change him, and Lord knows that I have tried!
My heart has been awakened to his deceptions and his lies.

He told me that he loved me, used to say I was his Boo!
He used to look into my eyes, the way you often do!
And, every time I see him now, he looks at me all wild.
I close my eyes sometimes and think, "I'm talking with a child"!

Girl, where's the man that I thought we had,
The man who'd be your Dad.
The dream that used to be forever,
Is not the one we have!

Now Baby, don't be scared because your mommy has no fears!
My motor's always running, and we're
about to change our gears!
It's you and mommy baby, and we're about to change our lane.
Your father isn't with us, but we will see him again!

He thinks about himself these days, but this is all about us!
So grab my hand young lady, and let's get up on this bus!
We're going to travel downtown, and
we're going to see the Judge.
He is very influential, so he'll make your father budge!

And when we get back home, I promise, we'll play in the park.
This shouldn't take too long; we should be home before it's dark!
But, if by chance, we find that we are walking with the moon,
We'll gather all your dolls and we will play up in your room.

And when it's time for bed, we'll both
lie down to read your book.
And maybe, you and I will talk about the trip we took!
And when we both are tired, we'll say prayers and go to sleep.
And you will dream of rainbows, while
your mommy's counting sheep!

Cherish

(A letter to my dance partner)

Cherish is a word I use to describe
The feelings I have, when I look in your eyes.
My words cannot capture these things of my heart—
The loss that I feel when our souls are apart.

See, each time I'm with you, I'm wanting you more!
My heart screams out "stay" as you walk out the door!
I look at the phone and expect it to ring.
Just the sound of your voice makes my heart start to sing!

I long to be with you, the touch of your skin.
Descriptions of feelings, oh how to begin!
I rise with the sun and my thoughts turn to you.
I'm so deeply in Love; I don't know what to do!

I look at your picture as I go through my day.
I'm so grateful to God, 'cause He blessed me this way!
And so, as we walk down this path we call life,
I'm counting my blessings— the first is my wife!

I don't take for granted, all the things that you bring
To the soul of this man; how you've taught it to sing.
So this is my promise, with this song that's of you.
I will cherish this dance, through the rhythms - and blues!

Yours—Truly!

Maybe

As I lay me down to sleep
Ms. Casey's on my mind.
We departed not so long ago
And confusion's what I find.

Seems every time I'm with her
It's my money or her pills.
And I feel like such a misfit
As I watch her do her deals.

"I'll only be two minutes",
I have heard so many times.
And there I'll sit inside my truck
As she leaves my world behind.

I wish sometime she'd hear my voice
And respect the way I feel.
She won't give me a second thought
'Cause she loves the way she feels.

And liquor seems her substitute
When she wants to feel real free.
Oh how I wish the day would come
When Casey chooses Me!

So today I feel a loser.
I was easily cast away.
"Big Daddy I want what I want",
Are the words I'll hear her say.

I'm sleepy now; I'll go lay down
'Cause the time is almost four.
I'll just climb back in my lonely bed
And I'll dream of her once more.

Ms. Clementine

When I was coming up in Queens—
When I was almost nine.
There was a lady in the hood
We called Ms. Clementine.

She wore weird boots and simple clothes—
A hat way out of time.
She wasn't very pretty!
And she wasn't very kind!

"Don't bother me!", she used to yell.
"You kids leave me alone!"
She lived inside a run-down house—
She lived there all alone!

We kids would always pick at her.
I guess that made her mean!
We'd kick her door; we'd ring her bell—
"Go way! - Go way!" she'd scream.

She never had a moment's peace
When we were on the street.
At night we'd throw a rock or two
To make our nights complete!

Ms. Clementine, she passed away
When I was just fifteen.
From that day on our lives would change
From things we had not seen.

Ms. Clementine was not so poor—
Not poor at all they said.
She left the world a will behind
And this is what it said!

To all the kids upon my street
I'd like to leave a gift.
Ten thousand dollars to each one.
And each one she did list!

I know they're good, the will went on.
They were just being kids!
And though they always did me wrong
I saw the good they did!

To me, the kids were just afraid
Because they could not see
That when I did the things I did
I was just being me!

See, though I walked a different path
Then everyone expected;
A human being's what I was
I should have been respected!

So, to these kids I leave this gift
With hopes that they'll soon see
That everyone in life deserves
Respect and Dignity!

I'm Sorry

I formed again some tears last night
From thoughts that filled my head!
I pictured all the gestures
And remembered words we said!

My mind retraced the path we took
To get us to this place.
Could not remember all the steps,
But sometimes saw mistakes!

To love the way I used to feel
When you came to my mind!
How stupid and naive I was
The times I was unkind!

Remembered how you held my hand—
Our fingers intertwined!
My Queen would step before me
And then, I would step behind!

We'd talk all day about nothings
And at night we'd do the same!
The sorrow that my heart feels now—
A minute to refrain!

"I'm sorry" does not measure up.
This depth cannot compare!
The thought that I could lose your love—
My heart begins to tear!

Please, tell me, what I need to do.
My life stands still in time!
I pray all day and more at night,
Forgiveness you might find!

I tried to call your phone last night—
Not meant to disrespect!
I hoped that we might share the line—
Our path we could reflect!

I fear that if you take too long,
And time— it comes to pass,
Your heart might turn away from me
And start another path!

"Please don't do that", my heart will cry.
I beg on broken knee!
I took for granted what we had
But now, I've come to see!

I see how much you loved me
Though the words I could not say!
I fell short in how I honored you.
So I bow to you this day!

I don't want to be your jester.
In my kingdom, you're my Queen!
I declare to you this solemn day
I will take my place as King!

If you come back to my kingdom,
I will love you all my days!
Never question how I love you!
Or ask, let me count the ways!

I will love you all tomorrows!
I will love you all todays!
I will stand in love of what we have—
Not a hint of yesterdays!

So, if you find me worthy,
Would you answer one more call?
I pray that as you do reflect
You see sunshine on your walls!

I dare not gamble on my chance
To win your heart again!
My only hope seems on my knees
Your forgiveness I could win!

And if you can't pick up your phone—
No connection to my tone!
I can only hope this way I feel
Will be mine and mine alone!

For no man's meant to suffer;
And no heart should feel this way!
I wish that I had said the words
I feel in my today!

"I am sorry" may not be enough
To win your heart again!
I am desperate for the love we had—
Won't believe— I've lost my friend!

Wait for Me

It is hard to see tomorrow
Through the dark of my today.
I look for mental pictures--
Confirmation I should stay!

Will no one touch my soul today?
Before my eve's arrived?
Or will this be like yesterday
Where no one's even tried!

A man of no significance.
How did this come to be?
I never thought my life would be
The way it is for me!

I've spent so many lonely nights;
The end to lonely days.
I believe that if I died tonight
No visits to my grave!

I'm like the dead man walking.
There's no hope on my green mile!
I walk my days with little hope
I'd be on somebody's mind!

For where do I find purpose
For my soul when I'm alone?
No answers to my call for change
No dial tone on my phone!

I know there's someone out there
Who could lend a helping hand.
Please don't give up your search for me!
And don't ever close your hand!

I'll get through this day somehow,
My constant morning prayer.
And if you'll keep your hand out,
There's a day that I'll be there!

So hope will walk beside me,
That's the thing I'll hold to fast!
And I will keep my eye out
For that hand that I can grasp!

I Was...

I'm a VICTIM, of my situation.
High blood pressure, low circulation—
Nobody seems to know my pain.
Nobody sees I'm going insane!

I'M A VICTIM! Of my circumstances.
No sympathies and no second chances—
Oh, why is it that no one sees.
This isn't how it's supposed to be!

I'M A VICTIM! I have no direction.
When sorrow rains, I have no protection!
I'm just a man, who's lost his way,
Just waiting for a better day.

I'M A VICTIM! Who's trying to be strong
When most my life has gone all wrong.
I pray for sunshine most my days,
But darkness seems to have its way!

I'M A VICTIM! Please hear me yell!
I'm looking for someone who'll help!
I've fallen; why does no one see,
That a victim, I don't want to be.

I'M A VICTIM! I don't want to lose
Won't turn to drugs, won't turn to booze.
I need to make a change this day!
It has to come from me! - They say!

I'M A VICTIM! But I won't be for long!
I will change my tune, so I'll change my song!
I've got to come out from this rain.
No longer can I stand this pain!

I'M A VICTIM! But I have my faith.
I know that I can change my fate!
Through God's love, I will find my way.
He'll change my life so I can Say…

I WAS A VICTIM, but I am no longer.
Found my path and now I'm stronger.
I no longer walk with my head low.
See, there's a God I've come to know!

I WAS A VICTIM, but I've changed my story!
I know God's love, so I know God's glory!
Gave Him my life; He's changed my days!
He's blessed me so I will never say!

I'M A VICTIM!

Good Bye, Old Friend

With every lashing of your tongue
You broke my spirit down.
And here I thought this thing we had
Could never come unbound.

You spoke of broken expectations
Of an event that was your own!
I suffered like some pauper
Who was knelt before your throne.

For who am I; this loner
You would cast upon such strife?
To give to you this Birthday wish
You have wanted for Your Life!

I am not your humbled servant
Nor a master of disguise.
I am just a lonely traveler
Who had thought he found a dime!

I guess our journey's ended
There's a fork now on this road.
I will hand your ass this nickel
For the debt you think I owe.

Please let me share this final thought
To the friend I had in you.
For the years our walk showed steps of four
And the times there were just two.

For the times when we walked through the rain
In the joys of me and you.
For the way your friendship made me feel
When the sun came shining through!

Please, let me state, before we part
That I love you all the same.
That I'm Thankful for the times we've had
And I hope we'll meet again.

Did You...

Did you see the sun rise this morning?
Did you witness its splendor?
Did you rise to the sound of the crack of dawn,
As it declared a new day has risen?
Did you meet with God to thank him for your blessings?
Did you reach for Him in your morning stretch?
Did you hear the trees as they called your name?
Did you smell the wind at its finest hour?

I've smelled the wind, I've met the sun, and I've wakened with my God!
I've risen before the early bird; I've even caught his worms!
Without a doubt, I can confess, I've looked upon God's blessings!
And when I lay me down to sleep, I know he holds my soul in the palms of His hands!

I will not take for granted, those things which speak of Him!
For, I have come to realize that, my life is not really my own.
It's merely a manifestation of His spoken word!

And God said...

Daydream

Have you ever stared in space?
Allowed what's real to be replaced?
At first you're here, but now you're gone,
Allowed what's real to be transformed.

To back away from all that's real
Sometimes reflect on how you feel!
A special place from all that's now
Never taught, you just know how!

You sit, you stare, and soon you find
That where you are is in your mind!
Allowed a place to let things go;
Allowed a place to let dreams flow!

It's just a dream, it won't last long.
It's just a note in life's sweet song.
Oh, what a place this world could be,
If to our dreams, we held the key!

Beyond the Thickets

She struggles so, this friend of mine-
Opinion of my soul.
Her lifestyle not reflective of
The stories she has told!

She seems to see a future
Success past what she shows.
I see her life in thickets deep
And she speaks of the rose!

The hope I have for my dear friend
Who walks with lessened time;
That she might come to see her dream.
The rose, I hope she finds!

Some say I am a foolish man
To hold to her so fast.
"You can't control her future",
But then, They don't know My past!

I think about the life I've had.
Some say I have success!
But there've been days, both near and far,
My life was filled with stress.

I've cried, at times, on bended knee.
Salvation from my woes.
I've lain amongst those thickets too!
I could not see the rose!

So who am I to turn my page
With not a lesson learned?
Those times, back then, have come to pass.
These roses I have earned!

As foolish as they say I am.
I'll walk beside my friend.
I'll lay before her petals
Till her thickets come to end!

And I may get a scratch or two.
May bleed from all my toes!
I have to walk beside my friend
Till she can smell the rose!

And if the time it takes my friend-
Her circumstance too deep.
I pray she'll walk through heaven's gate
With roses at her feet!

Curtain Call

She fights a battle everyday
For whom she'd have you see.
She hides behind her theatre masks
To hide the shame she feels.

She gets up every morning
And with mirror counts her flaws.
She'll hide behind her theatre masks
So we can't see her scars.

Her scars are not of mere skin tone.
She hasn't had a fight.
Her scars have formed an armored coat
She lives in day and night.

Her pains are not outside her
For they dwell from deep inside.
And every day as she awakes
She thinks of ways to hide.

"I wish that I were pretty",
She feels deep inside her mind.
She looks for ways to fix her flaws
And better ways to hide.

Her memories lie down with her.
And with morning comes a new.
This child of God has nightmares
Of what life has put her through.

Her todays are just like yesterdays.
And tomorrow's hopes soon dash
As thoughts plant seeds of yesteryear
Saying, "This is all you'll have!"

And when we see her on the street
She will smile and say "Hello!"
For with morning comes the curtain's rise
And her mind says, "Start the show!"

Declaration of Love

Thank You, for the joyful noise,
The times of days now past.
Thank You, for the memories;
They're the ones my heart now grasps.

The years are many; you held my hand.
I've never been alone.
We've shared a love, a walk, a time.
Our house is now our home.

And though there're times I do forget
The left hand to the right,
I'm mindful now, of days gone by;
How you've become my light!

How blessed my life has come to be.
Oh, how I reminisce.
I'm mindful of the way I felt.
You gave me my first kiss.

These days you may not hold my hand.
And kisses, now, are few!
I would not have a moment changed
No Me without a You!

So on this day, with God beside
I reminisce on life.
That day we kissed, you held my hand
Declared, "Husband and Wife".

A Man on the Water

The boat's in the water.
The sun's in your eyes.
The wind whispers "go!"
And the bow starts to rise.

The motor is humming
And the gas tank is full.
You start to have visions
Of the fish that you'll pull.

No chatter amongst you
As you take in the wind.
You prepare for the spot
Where the fishing begins.

And as the boat slows
And the boat starts to rest,
Someone tosses the anchor
And the moment is set.

The reels start a spinning
And the stories spin too.
There are stories of conquests
That are mostly, not true!

But a man on the water
Is a man who is free.
It's just him and his comrades
On the big open sea.

They will talk of occasions
When they've gathered before.
They will laugh at each other
And oh so much more!

At the end of the day
As the bow starts to rise.
And the sun starts to set
They'll reflect on their prize.

But it's not of their fish—
Not the ones caught or lost.
They'll reflect on their friendships—
Maybe friends that they've lost.

They'll reflect on their Families,
On the day that they had.
They'll reflect on the good days
And reflect on the bad.

And as the bow lowers
And the pier comes aside,
They'll hug each one dearly
And proceed to their rides.

A man on the water
Is a man who is free.
The sun in his face
On the big open sea.

'Til He Snores and He Moans

Her heart cries out wildly.
It's the threat of his tone.
It's the words that he'll say—
Like, "I'll break every bone!"

She just wants him to love her
Like she sees with her peers—
Hold his daughter with passion
Not to bring her to tears!

But her father is broken
From his days far behind—
Doesn't know how to love her
He can't even be kind!

Cigarettes and a bottle
He consumes between breaths.
And he's blamed his poor daughter
'Cause her Mother has left!

She must speak to him softly—
Must not rattle his cage.
'Cause the beast will come out
With his anger and rage!

So, she feeds him his beers
And he sits and he groans.
She attends to his needs
'Til he snores and he moans.

Here's her moment of peace
In this house, that's her home.
But her heart cries out softly
While she suffers alone!

Not a moment is blissful
In her moments in time.
No one sees how she suffers—
To her world, they're all blind!

She will go through the motions
That will hide her from sight.
No one knows of her wanting—
How she begs for some light!

Her life, caught in the turmoil
Of a life not her own.
This poor child of a monster
Who gives peace when he moans!

Beauty is the Beast

They say that beauty's in the eye
Of the one who shall behold.
No common ground can beauty have
Since each one has their own.

So when I speak of beauty,
Would you, please, respect the eye
And see that there's no judgment
So no YOU can be applied!

I see beauty at the water's edge
With the glow of new day's rise.
I see beauty in the dead of night
As I peer toward starlit skies!

Behold the things around you—
How each one does have its place!
And realize that beauty
Is much deeper than one's face!

How beautiful a life could be
Without egoic eye!
When we refuse to judge someone
Whose mold does not apply!

When never do we query
'Bout the look, the size, the skin;
When there is no need for mirrors
As our new days do begin!

We have to wonder how it was
We came to see this way!
When what somebody thinks of you
Is judged by someone's taste!

For what's the measure of a man
If not by his own view?
They should look into their mirrors first
Before they look at you!

Allow no man to set the tone
For how you feel about you!
You're the best that you can be, right now!
Let no man measure you!

Stand tall in how you are today
Avoid the looking glass!
Don't stand for some egoic rule
No measure shall they have!

Your truth is what you see in self.
Let no man have this measure!
Stand tall in who you are this day
And know that you're the treasure!

Girls Night Out for Daddy

The attempt is mine to bring to light
These words she will not hear;
To ward off all the planted seeds
That root in silent fear.

To do no wrong, her quest may be,
But blinded eyes they do not see.
And conscience walks with no man
Who can only think of thee.

How does a Dad convey to child
The essence of concern?
When child has not the eyes to see
The scars of lessons learned.

He loves her so, his blessed child-
The apple of his eyes.
He'll smile upon her golden shine
While fear lay deep inside.

"Don't go that way!" he'll say to her
Remembering what has been.
The cautions of a father's love
To ward off evil's grin.

But, oh his child of little light-
To her the road seems bright.
She'll wave him off and take the path-
Her heart so full of spite.

And many paths his child will choose
Temptation as her guide.
She'll dance the night in devilish brace
With blinders on her eyes.

What does a father say to child
Who means so much to him?
When Daddy has remembrance of
The paths of which he's been?

"Don't choose that road!" I've been before.
"It's not the one for you!"
"I must see for myself dear Dad,
This is the one I choose!"

And so, the Dad will sit and wait.
He'll listen by the phone-
In hopes that silent stays the ring
Until his daughter's home.

His child will stay out in the night;
Throw caution to the wind.
While Daddy's mind is swept in thoughts
Of devil's tempting sin.

And then his daughter enters home
With taste of devil's wine.
And yells out to her confidants
"Let's go again some time!"

That quick relief that Daddy felt
Is thrown out with the wind.
Because Daddy knows, it won't be long-
He'll go through this again!

It's at this point that Daddy's heart
Falls down below his knees.
And Daddy mumbles silent prayers
Like, "NOT AGAIN LORD, PLEASE!"

Then Daddy, with his swollen heart,
Looks into Princess eyes.
Will say to her, in jaded jest,
"I hope you had good times!"

"Of course I did", she'll say to Dad.
With not one detail more,
She'll go off to her Princess room
And close her Princess door.

The Invisible Man

Who is this man who has loved from his heart,
Who is there for his loves, when their lives fall apart?
He will come to their rescue, with an "S" on his chest,
When his loyalties questioned, he aces the test!

Who is this man, who will give of himself?
Who will stand by your side when there's nobody else?
He will give of his time, of his money; His creed...
"I'm here when you need me, just call on me, Please!"

This man who will council, who will lend you his ear,
Who will pray for your soul, if it's death that you fear.
Who is this man that will carry your load,
Who will walk your life with you, and your hand he will hold?

Who is this man with his heart full of love?
He's a passionate man with his sights from above.
And who is this man who'll consider your needs,
Who'll remember your soul, when he's down on his knees?

And who is this man who has given his all,
Who has vowed to be there-- if ever you call?
And who is this man that has swallowed his pride
When you've said things to hurt him, and pushed him aside?

Who is this man who has felt all alone,
Who's expected a letter, a ring on the phone?
Who is this man who has suffered in pain,
Been betrayed by his loved ones, again and again?

He's a man who will sacrifice all that he is,
Who will give of his life, so his children can live.
He will sacrifice all-- for the sake of his soul;
He's a man who lives, looking, for hands he can hold.

He can't give you answers for all life may bring,
But when your soul's hurting, you can give him a ring.
This man is no hero, so he shall win no prize;
He's a man who sees God, when he looks in your eyes.

He's a man on a quest to seek God, and seek love,
Who will dust himself off, every time that you shove.
Please don't take for granted his compassion for weak.
It's not your attention; it's God's love that he seeks.

The invisible man—how he wishes you'd see
The struggles he's had, yet he's still on his feet.
The invisible man—he wants much for himself,
But will sacrifice most days, for somebody else.

He longs to be seen for the things he has done,
For the trials that he's faced-- for the battles he's won.
He doesn't want flowers, no birthday surprise;
He wants you to see him, when you look in his eyes.

He doesn't want much—the invisible man;
Just show him some love-- every chance that you can!
And when you are lonely and feeling real sad
He'll be right there beside you; he'll be holding your hand.

No, you may not see him, 'cause you haven't thus far,
But you do know his name, and you do know his heart!
The invisible man—He is true to the game.
And though you don't see him—you will see him again!

I Has a Proposal. . .

The "I" that I am to me, would like the "you" that you are to it, to understand that it has sole responsibility for the "I" that it is to itself.

"I" understands the pressure that the "you" that you are to it constantly puts itself under in trying to understand the "you" that I am to you. "I" understands that the "you" that you are to me believes that, it is 'more informed' about things that my "I" is experiencing in its journey. Your "I" seems to suggest that it is so informed about the things of life, which can only be truly experienced in its "I", that it wants my "I" to believe it knows what is best for my "me". In all reality, however, the "you" that you are to me is the only "I" that can be found in the "you" that we both know. The way I sees it, your "I" can only have experiences and thus, responsibility for the "you" that your "I" is to me. All "I's" control their experiences through their own "I's" based on decisions they make for themselves. So let's You and I have this understanding. . .

"I" will worry about itself and "You" can mind its business.

What do you think???

A Good Morning

The sun rises slowly
And your day soon begins.
You tilt your head back
As you capture the wind.

The temperature changes
As the sun starts to rise—
The orange, the yellow
So bright to your eyes!

As you bask in its glory,
Its splendor, its grace.
You close both your eyes
And you give it your face.

It's you and it's nature
As the birds come along.
They seem nestled around you
And they sing you their songs.

How simple the moment.
How it touches your soul.
What a glorious day!
A new day to behold!

The trees start a swaying
And the leaves start to wave.
The sun rises higher
And your spirit is raised.

To bask in His glory
Is a gift to your soul.
Each moment is blissful
You want more to unfold!

But it's just a beginning.
It's a spark to your life.
It's not your forever—
But, for now, it's so right.

You'll push back your chair
And you'll gather your things.
'Cause you know it's not long
Before your phone starts to ring!

Holding On

Would anyone miss me if I died?
Can anyone sense the tears inside?
Esteem that's melted from my heart
Replaced by dreams of a new start.

Can anyone I once called a friend
Detect my journey may soon end?
Oh why, My Lord, does no one see?
The way my life has come to be!

I'm lost in life; I'm lost in love.
My only strength is from above.
A hug, a kiss, why don't they see—
The little things are all I need!

I feel my life has lost its flare.
And no one around me seems to care!
I cry inside from day to day—
Will someone please love Me today!

If not for love of life, and God
I don't think I could carry on!
And so, I show my happy face
Though in my heart I feel misplaced.

I hold to things I hope exist—
In hopes one day to have my wish.
For someone close to sense my plight—
To grab my hand and hold it tight.

I pray someone will come today
Who'll realize, I've lost my way!
Someone who'll grab me by the hand
And say to me, "I understand!"

Forbidden Dance

Here I sit my eyes full of the reality that has defined our friendship. My heart pounds hard and heavy as the thought of life without you plays through my mind like an old black and white movie.
Every breath I take sends vibes throughout my soul; vibes which are reminiscent of the fact that my heart is now broken. I wonder, can we try again? Can we return to the old days, the old ways, the feelings, the laughter, the special times that belong to you and I alone?

We were not lovers, yet we loved. We could not be separated, yet we belonged to other people. Our hearts, though they beat to a different drum, still played a rhythm that became our song, our tune. We were one, if only for a piece of time, as we danced in friendship's ballroom. Our dance was a short waltz, which played life's beat for those who love from a distance. Seems now our dance has ended.

I will miss you dance partner.

Hopeful

I know you won't remember me
Like I remember you.
I keep your picture in my mind.
Today, I'm scrolling through!

My memory has this vision
Of a time I've held in place.
It brings a feeling to my heart
And a smile upon my face.

Most times I see you in my nights;
We share a glimpse or two.
And on those nights you're in my arms;
I wake with thoughts of you!

We shared a brief encounter;
A reality far too small.
I hold this memory in my soul
Though your name I can't recall!

But names are not important
Until my wish has come to pass;
When you and I are hand in hand
Just strolling down life's path.

Today you're just a vision
Of a time that's from our past.
So, if my prayers don't bring you back
I pray this vision lasts!

I Know — How

I lay in bed this morning.
I reflected on my now.
And joyous was my heart right then
Remembering all my Hows.

How will I get through this thing?
I could not see the light.
And How can I keep standing?
How will I win this fight!

I remembered How I loved you.
And How our babies came.
The biggest How I ever had—
Oh, How my life was changed!

The Hows, for now, have come to pass-
At least for my today!
Oh How I am so thankful—
How I've seemed to find a way!

So, How are you today, my friend?
I'll ask throughout this day
For a testimonial of your past—
Or the joy of your today!

I Wish

I wish that I could see beyond
These trees that sky before me.
This path, so dark, so little light
Unknown that keeps me weary.

Confusion walks here with me—
Not always by my side.
Sometimes it walks before me;
Sometimes it walks behind.

But none the less, I'll keep my stride
Like all who've walked before me.
And like them all, I hope that I
Will leave a happy story.

A tale of strength, of hope, of praise
For all the world to see.
And in the end, I hope it says
That this man did succeed!

Mall Chicks

"She thinks she's so cute!" I hear in your mood.
Don't think I don't hear because your lips haven't moved!
It's all in your gestures, the slant of your eyes.
You thought you were cute and then my ass walked by!

Yeah, I've got your man, he is in my control.
And you can't believe that it's his gaze I hold.
Girl, all men are dogs and we women their masters.
I don't have a leash, but I see that you have to!

You're angry with me because his eyes have been gazing?
Seems now, I'm the one your man wishes he'd been chasing!
Girl, take your man home, let him play with his bone!
And the next time you come, honey, leave him at home!

You think because he walks with you, close by your side
Your man's being good, because he's matching your strides?
Girl, his eyes have been roaming since you both hit this mall.
From corner to corner, your old man's seen us all!

Oh yeah, I'm the dish he now has on his mind.
His talk might be yours, but his thoughts are all mine!
Girl, it's not your fault that your man acts this way!
He just needs to be trained, what more can I say?

Oh honey, don't fret, because I don't want your stray!
I'll just shoot him this gesture; this will send him your way!
But don't think it's over, all the panting and whine!
At home he's all yours, but in here, he's all mine!

My Tribute to Senior Citizens

I used to celebrate my birthdays
Until I got too old;
When candles on my cake would serve
As shelter from the cold!

Yes, I remember Valentine's
We'd all confess our love!
Seems love is over-rated now
Because now it's just a hug!

And oh the joys of Easter
When we kids would hide our eggs!
You hide an egg from Mama now,
She'll go up side your head!

And Christmas – I remember when
Our tree was filled with gifts!
But all good gifts have been replaced
With gift certificates!

And I remember New Years!
How the parties used to rock!
Now, I leave it up to others
I'm in bed by Nine o'clock!

Don't think my life is boring
Because my story's fallen short!
These candles are like medals
They all tell a tale of sort!

To be a senior citizen,
An honor to my peers!
It means we've stood the test of time
And triumphed through the years!

See, many soldiers trudge through time
Some have fallen in the ranks.
And we who carry on today
Deserve a bit of thanks!

For we have kept the Family Tree
Intact, so it will grow!
I understand your ignorance child!
There are things you just don't know!

So, while you count my candles
And you hold your mouth in awe.
I will wallow in my grandest pride!
See, I brought us this far!

My Hope

I cry inside my lonely soul
The things that break my heart.
The words my mind may call upon
To break my whole apart.

I know I'm not alone in this;
These words they speak of all.
To feel alone with thoughts of God
The life line left to call.

For no one knows the way I feel
Because my voice won't speak.
I've fallen so far deep inside
Yet no one sees I'm weak!

Will no one come to lend an ear
Behind my risen wall?
My life line feels of disconnect
'Cause no one comes to call!

I suffer through this disconnect -
My mind so filled with doubt.
Will someone come unlock this vault?
And help my soul get out!

At times I've come to realize
This walk is mine alone.
It's up to me to break this wall—
To reconnect my phone!

And, if I reach inside myself,
Will you help me climb this wall?
And if I reconnect this line,
Is it you that I can call?

Do you see me in your mirror?
Do you feel these words I speak?
Will you look inside my broken heart?
Not continue just to peek!

For loud is not the voice I have
As I suffer through my pain.
Can I count on you to see beyond
All the scars for what remains?

When you've felt the touch of broken soul
Will you help connect the call?
Will you listen for my soulful cry?
Put you ear up to my wall?

Will you look inside my eyes with love--
When it's you who's put me down?
Can we reconnect through loving eyes?
Send me love without a sound?

I know you can; I hope you will.
It's your words I need to hear.
Put your arms around my lonely soul.
Give me comfort through my fears!

And when the time has come to pass—
When I've come through all my trials.
Will you hear the tones of reconnect
When my heart begins to smile!

It's my hope that you will know God's love
So we can both meet soul to soul.
That it's you who's helped me find the way
To make my life feel whole!

On Her Behalf

One New York day with sun aglow
With blinded eyes I did behold
The plight a woman's life became-
A life I felt had turned to shame!

This woman, who was dark of skin,
And also short of stature,
Had roped a life, I do believe
God meant no man to capture!

Her eyes ablaze; her gate a stagger
She'd lost all pride, it did not matter.
To most, she must have seemed a hag
To walk the streets in plastic bag!

Unto my heart I felt a pain.
My eyes a tear, could not refrain-
To see how drugs had took control
Of everything that made her whole.

I did not know her name or purpose-
Wasn't mine to see!
But through my soul, I felt her pain,
And so, I pray to thee.

I pray, oh God, you'd grab her soul
And come into her heart.
Please help my sister break away
And come out from the dark!

For all who walk with God beside
Shall come to see His glory.
Lord, help my sister come to see
She can re-write her story!

Plastic People

"Merry Christmas!" - " Happy New Year!"
That's what they always yell!
But what do those words mean to those
Whose life's a living hell!

We live on streets and on the train
Amongst the stench and rubble;
And every year, about the end
Come people from the bubble.

See, all year long they walk right by you,
Shake their heads from left to right.
They act as if they've read a book
That tells about your life.

"He's given up! She's just a bum!"
These words come to their minds.
And here we are at this year's end
And now they're acting kind?

You'll touch me now, but not before,
You want to ease my pain?
When just last month you walked right by
While I froze in the rain!

Don't come to help me at year's end
As if you have compassion!
You put on airs at Christmas time
As if it's some new fashion.

I know my life is not the way
You'd really like to see.
But you should spend time in my shoes
Instead of your TV!

What you see is not real life
For those who live the streets!
For most of us, there's something wrong;
Our lives are not complete!

Happy New Year, Merry Christmas,
Just don't mean a thing
When those words come from those who'll soon-
WALK PAST US IN THE RAIN.

She Stood Outside the Walmart

She stood outside the Walmart
Her kids played by her side!
The look upon this mother's face
Who stood without her pride!

She held a sign that asked for food
A tattered cardboard strip.
As passersby would catch her life
Her struggle met her lips!

As I approached her weary soul
I struggled with her too!
I put myself in Mama's place
Did what she had to do!

To beg for food this Arab woman
Dressed in Arab garb.
With knowledge of the prejudice felt
Toward Arabs must be hard!

This thing, she did, she struggled through
Could see it crushed her soul!
She reached for every car that passed
For something she could hold.

I wondered – is this meant to be?
The struggles and the fights!
Is this how God would have us be?
Since He –"let there be light!"

Why is it - just at Christmas time
Some see with open heart?
And why is it - just Christmas time
We try to do our part?

"Tis the season", are the words
Some utter at this time.
Then as the season passes through
Compassion's hard to find!

Why is it - we can't come together
Stand beneath " His" flag!
And wave it proudly all life long
No judgement - to be had!

Why can't we comfort - one and all
Embrace each one in kind?
Give rest to weary travelers
And feel blessed in what we find!

Sometimes

Sometimes you love me,
And sometimes you don't
Sometimes you'll hug me,
And sometimes you won't.

It seems as if "sometimes",
Is all you can give.
I'm a fool who thinks "always"
Is how we should live.

I try to appease you,
I'll give you your space,
"Don't want to be bothered"
I'll see on your face.

You see since "I Love You",
I'll take it in stride,
It's ups and downs always,
Like some sort of ride.

I'll never let go of—
Those times that we've had.
Those times you were happy.
Those times you were sad.

I've come to see sometimes
You give what you can.
I offer you <u>Always</u>
Your friend to the end.

Made in the USA
Columbia, SC
27 March 2018